SCIENCE QUEST

The Search for

Food Breakthroughs

by Clint Twist

GARETH**STEVENS**
GS
PUBLISHING
A WRC Media Company

Please visit our web site at: www.garethstevens.com
For a free color catalog describing Gareth Stevens Publishing's list of high-quality books
and multimedia programs, call 1-800-542-2595 (USA) or 1-800-387-3178 (Canada).
Gareth Stevens Publishing's fax: (414) 332-3567.

Library of Congress Cataloging-in-Publication Data

Twist, Clint.
    The search for food breakthroughs / by Clint Twist. — North American ed.
       p. cm. — (Science quest)
    Includes index.
    ISBN 0-8368-4555-2 (lib. bdg.)
    1. Food industry and trade—Juvenile literature. I. Title. II. Series.
  TP370.3.T88   2005
  664—dc22   2004059149

This North American edition first published in 2005 by
Gareth Stevens Publishing
A WRC Media Company
330 West Olive Street, Suite 100
Milwaukee, WI 53212 USA

This U.S. edition copyright © 2005 by Gareth Stevens, Inc. Original edition copyright © 2004 by ticktock Entertainment Ltd.
First published in Great Britain in 2004 by ticktock Media Ltd., Unit 2, Orchard Business Centre, North Farm Road, Tunbridge Wells,
Kent, TN2 3XF.

Gareth Stevens editor: Carol Ryback
Gareth Stevens designer: Kami M. Koenig

Photo Credits: (t=top, b=bottom, c=center, l=left, r=right)
Alamy: 2–3, 4–5, 7(t), 8(t), 20(l), 25(br), 26(l), 26–27(tc), 27(br). Anthony Blake: 12(c), 14(b), 20–21(t), 21(r), 24(l), 25(t),
25(b), 28–29(tc), 29(br). CORBIS: 5 (all), 8(b), 10–11(c), 14–15(c), 15(t), 16(c). Science Photo Library: 9(b), 11(r), 14(l),
17(r), 22–23(c), 23(r), 28(c). Still Pictures: 16(b).

Printed in the United States of America

1 2 3 4 5 6 7 8 9 09 08 07 06 05

Contents

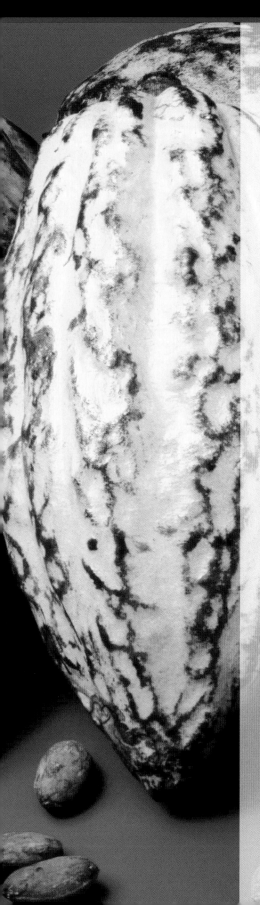

Words that appear in the glossary are printed in
boldface type the first time they occur in the text.

Introduction

ood **technologists** are scientists who usually work behind the scenes. Although their profession might seem mysterious, we are all familiar with the results of their work. In fact, the chances are that food technologists somehow added to the flavor or **texture** of the food you just ate.

What Does a Food Technologist Do?

A food technologist works to improve the food we eat through careful and scientific control of the ingredients in food. Food technologists also try to make food safer, better tasting, healthier, longer lasting, and more exciting. They are constantly searching for new methods to improve foods and food processes. They might even invent "new" foods, such as **mycoprotein**, which is a popular meat substitute in some countries.

Chefs or Mechanics?

Some food technologists might easily be mistaken for chefs because they spend so much time in laboratories that look like kitchens. They often need to figure out the best ways to prepare, cook, store, and reheat good-tasting meals in large quantities. To mass-produce ready-made meals, food technologists must understand exactly how each of the ingredients behaves during every step of these different processes.

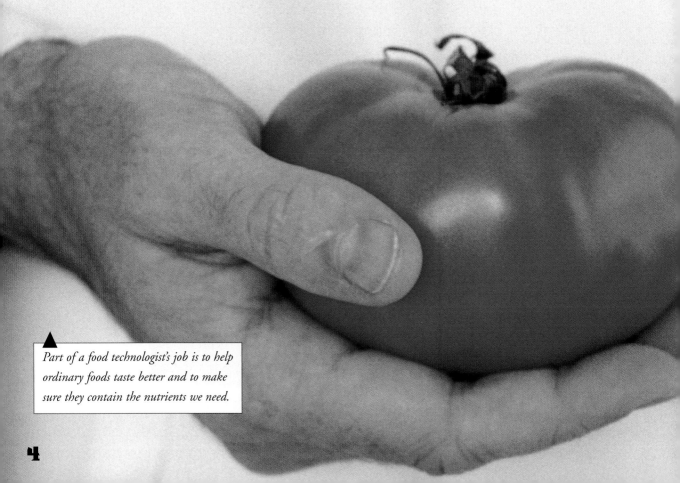

▲
Part of a food technologist's job is to help ordinary foods taste better and to make sure they contain the nutrients we need.

Food scientists spend hours in the laboratory creating exciting new flavors to stimulate the taste buds of consumers.

Some food technologists seem more like mechanics. They design and maintain the machines that are used to prepare foods. Some of these machines operate in surprising ways. Potatoes are often peeled by high-temperature steam and then cut into french fries by a high-speed water-gun knife.

Food technologists also work hard to make food fun to eat. They know how to make the smoothest chocolate, control the amount of fizz in sodas, and give pretzels, chips, and other snacks extra crunch. Some of the most important food technologists are flavor experts who may never actually see food in the course of a work day. They spend all their time in a laboratory combining different chemicals as they search for new and inexpensive ways to produce familiar flavors.

Keeping Us Healthy

Some food technologists seem more like health workers. They make sure our foods contain all the **vitamins** and **minerals** that keep us healthy. They also help people who, for various reasons, cannot eat certain ingredients. By using their scientific knowledge, food technologists can produce milk for **lactose-intolerant** people (those who cannot digest milk products) and sweet foods for people who must limit their sugar intake (**diabetics**).

A food scientist adds preservatives — chemicals that make food last longer — to peaches.

The Best Chocolate Ever

Chocolate is made from the ripe seeds of the cacao tree, which grows in the tropics. If you ate one of these seeds right off the tree, it would taste unpleasant. It takes a considerable amount of technology to turn these seeds — confusingly called cocoa beans — into chocolate, one of our favorite foods.

From the Tree

Harvested cocoa beans are piled in the hot sun for several days to **ferment**. Fermentation is a process that breaks down sugars into **carbon dioxide** gas and other chemicals. Fermenting the cocoa beans helps certain flavor-producing chemicals develop. The food industry also uses fermentation to make bread rise or to produce alcohol.

Fermented cocoa beans are roasted and ground into a powder. Most of the natural oil in the beans, called cocoa butter, is extracted (removed) during the grinding process. The dark mass that remains is a bitter-tasting substance that forms the basis for all chocolate and chocolate-flavored products.

Working the Mass

The ground-up chocolate mass serves as cocoa powder for use in hot drinks and as a baking ingredient. Chocolate mass for candy is warmed until it melts. Then food technologists add sugar and more oil, usually in the form of cocoa butter. Milk chocolate is made with either fresh, dried, or condensed milk. A substance called **lecithin** is added to help the ingredients blend together.

In the final process, called conching, machines beat the cocoa mixture constantly for up to three days. Conching makes the chocolate product very smooth when it cools and solidifies and gives the chocolate its excellent texture, or "**mouthfeel**."

SCIENCE CONCEPTS

A Good Mix

Lecithin, a soybean product, is a type of food ingredient known as an **emulsifier**. An emulsifier breaks up oils into small droplets that can mix with other liquids. It also prevents the oil droplets from sticking to each other, keeping the oil evenly distributed throughout the mixture, which is called an emulsion. Emulsifiers are used widely in the food industry.

These Ecuadorian cocoa pods are bursting with ripe beans that will eventually be turned into delicious chocolate.

Final Touches

After conching, other ingredients, such as fruit, nuts, or pieces of honeycombed sugar, may be added to the mixture before it is poured into molds to cool. Chocolate bars that contain two or more types of chocolate are made by pouring the chocolates into the molds one at a time.

Lecithin helps hold together the many different ingredients in this exotic chocolate bar.

SCIENCE SNAPSHOT

Part of chocolate's wonderful texture is a matter of simple physics. The melting point of chocolate is about 98.6° Fahrenheit (37° Celsius), which is the same temperature as the average human body. Its body-temperature melting point is the reason that chocolate (which is a solid at room temperature) begins to melt as soon as you pop it into your mouth or hold it very long.

Food becomes spoiled, stale, or rotten if it goes too long without being eaten. Food spoilage can happen very quickly if the natural packaging is removed or damaged, as when, for example, fruit and vegetables are peeled or become bruised. Bad food usually tastes unpleasant, and it can cause serious illnesses. Food technologists have developed several ways to make foods last longer.

How Food Goes Bad

Some foods, such as meat, fresh fruits, and fresh vegetables, can be spoiled by contact with the air. The food reacts with the **oxygen** gas in the air and begins to change color, as when a slice of apple or potato turns brown. This process is known as **oxidation**, which is the same thing that happens when iron rusts. The oxidization of food is not particularly dangerous, but it makes food look very unappetizing.

Dangerous Organisms

Millions of mostly harmless **microbes** live on our skin and in the air. Food is also a very good place for microbes, such as **bacteria** and **fungi**, to live. Some microbes are dangerous and multiply rapidly when they get into food. As they help the food rot, they produce poisonous waste products. Even tiny quantities of these poisons can make a person ill. Keeping food safe from microbes is one of the most important tasks for food technologists.

An apple left at room temperature for several days may begin to rot, especially if it is bruised.

SCIENCE CONCEPTS

Pasteurization

The **pasteurization** process makes fresh milk safe to drink. Milk is briefly heated to a high temperature and then quickly cooled. This process kills dangerous microbes, but not those that cause milk to spoil (even refrigerated milk will sour after a time). **Ultra-heat-treated** (UHT) milk is heated to an extreme temperature, then instantly cooled. UHT milk stays good for months without refrigeration.

Keeping It Safe

Perhaps the most common way to keep food fresh for long periods of time is by canning it. Meat, fruit, vegetables, and other foods can be kept safe this way. Raw food is sealed inside an airtight metal can and heated to kill any microbes. After the can cools, it can be safely stored for several years. Keeping food cool in a refrigerator can also slow the growth of microbes, but it does not stop it completely. Like all living things, microbes need water. They cannot grow without it. Food that has been completely dehydrated (dried) can be stored much longer than fresh food — but not all food is suitable for dehydration. Freezing foods can stop microbes from growing because the water is frozen into ice crystals. Proper cooking also kills microbes, but cooking is different from preserving food for storage.

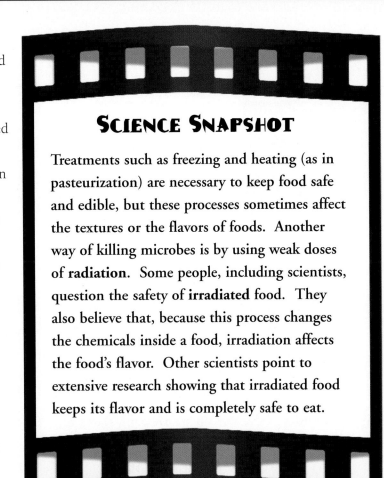

SCIENCE SNAPSHOT

Treatments such as freezing and heating (as in pasteurization) are necessary to keep food safe and edible, but these processes sometimes affect the textures or the flavors of foods. Another way of killing microbes is by using weak doses of **radiation**. Some people, including scientists, question the safety of **irradiated** food. They also believe that, because this process changes the chemicals inside a food, irradiation affects the food's flavor. Other scientists point to extensive research showing that irradiated food keeps its flavor and is completely safe to eat.

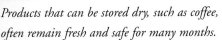

Products that can be stored dry, such as coffee, often remain fresh and safe for many months. ▶

Flavor is the main reason we prefer some foods and drinks to others. Strawberry is a very popular flavor, but not enough strawberries are grown to supply the demand. Some of the world's most skilled and talented food technologists work to create and blend flavors. They help make those flavors more available, often at less cost. In fact, the familiar tastes of many of the things we eat and drink are created in laboratories.

The human tongue has different places for tasting basic flavors.

What is Yummy?

Our sense of taste is more complicated than you may think. The taste buds on the tongue detect basic flavor characteristics, including sweet, sour, salty, and bitter, but testing a food on your outstretched tongue is not really tasting it. Taste buds act as a **defense mechanism** that prevents us from eating poisonous foods — which usually taste very bitter. To taste something properly, the food must be inside the mouth where flavor **molecules** can drift up to sense **receptors** in the nose. When we enjoy the flavors of food and drink, we are mainly using our sense of smell. Most substances have distinctive smells. They release molecules into the air that can be detected by sense receptors. Humans have a good sense of smell and can recognize thousands of different kinds of smells. Some smells are produced by one particular molecule, while others are a combination of many different molecules.

SCIENCE CONCEPTS

Flavoring

Food flavor is one of those areas of science where the difference between "natural" and "artificial" becomes blurred. In some cases, the difference is between two methods of producing the same chemicals. Most countries have strict regulations about the use of the words "flavor," "flavoring," and "flavored" on food labels.

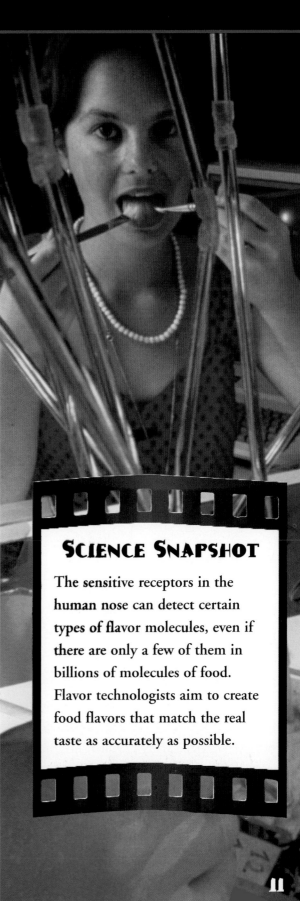

This food researcher is putting food chemicals on her tongue and writing down exactly the tastes she experiences.

Making a Flavor

Popular flavors, such as strawberry, orange, and chocolate, have been analyzed and broken down into their different chemical molecules. Once food technologists know exactly what makes a particular flavor, they can devise ways of using different ingredients to produce the same effect on the sense receptors. It can take more than three hundred different ingredients, mixed together in exactly the right combination, to produce an artificial strawberry flavor in a laboratory. Yet strawberry flavor is easier to make in a laboratory than the flavor of roasted meat. Technologists need nearly one thousand different ingredients to produce the flavor of roasted meat in a food laboratory.

Natural flavors such as orange, lemon, and strawberry can now be recreated easily in a laboratory.

SCIENCE SNAPSHOT

The sensitive receptors in the human nose can detect certain types of flavor molecules, even if there are only a few of them in billions of molecules of food. Flavor technologists aim to create food flavors that match the real taste as accurately as possible.

Substitute Foods

There are some common food ingredients, such as milk, wheat flour, and sugar, that many people cannot eat. It is not a matter of taste or liking. These particular foods can upset people's stomachs and can even make them very ill. Food technologists must be able to identify these ingredients so that foods can be correctly labeled. They also work hard to produce substitute foods that do not contain these ingredients.

Milk

Most people enjoyed drinking milk when they were children, but as adults, some may feel unwell after they drink milk. They have a condition known as lactose intolerance. Their digestive systems cannot process the kind of sugar, called lactose, found in animal milk. To help lactose-intolerant people enjoy a bowl of breakfast cereal with milk, technologists have developed substitute milks made from plant foods, such as soybeans, that do not contain lactose.

Wheat Flour

Some people cannot tolerate **gluten,** a substance found in the wheat flour, which is a main ingredient of bread, cookies, pasta, and many other food products. Rye flour also contains gluten, but rye flour is not as widely used as wheat flour. Food technologists can remove the gluten from some products during the food preparation process. A wide variety of gluten-free products, including baby foods, are now available.

Sugar

Many people suffer from an illness called **diabetes**. People with diabetes, who are known as diabetics, must keep track of how much sugar they eat. If they eat too much or too little sugar, they may become seriously ill. Diabetics must pay close attention to food labels because many food products contain sugar even if they do not taste sweet. Food technologists have developed a wide range of diabetic food substitutes that taste the same as ordinary foods. Chocolate for diabetics, for example, is often sweetened with fruit sugars, and carob beans may be used instead of the cocoa mass.

Carob beans contain natural sugars and are often used as a chocolate substitute.

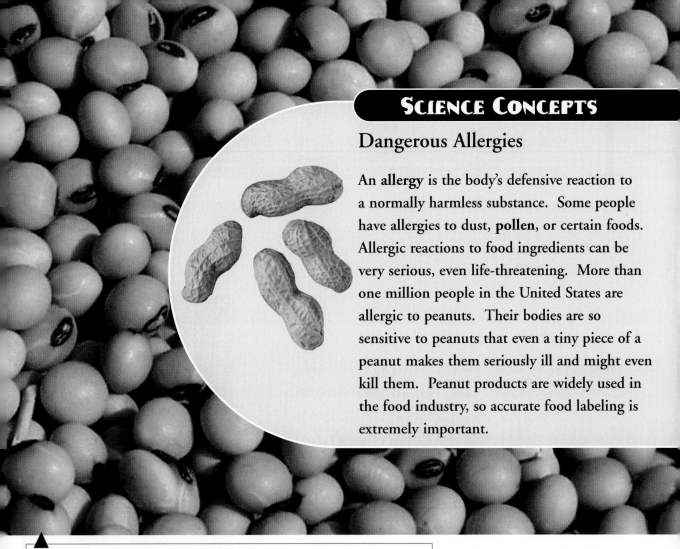

Dangerous Allergies

An **allergy** is the body's defensive reaction to a normally harmless substance. Some people have allergies to dust, **pollen**, or certain foods. Allergic reactions to food ingredients can be very serious, even life-threatening. More than one million people in the United States are allergic to peanuts. Their bodies are so sensitive to peanuts that even a tiny piece of a peanut makes them seriously ill and might even kill them. Peanut products are widely used in the food industry, so accurate food labeling is extremely important.

*Soybeans are grown in North and South America and in China. To help soybeans thrive, special types have been developed that are resistant to **herbicides**.*

SCIENCE SNAPSHOT

Food technologists are currently working on the peanut allergy problem. They are hoping to discover exactly which of the thirty or so chemicals in peanuts triggers allergic reactions. Once they have identified the cause of the problem, they will work to produce a "safe" peanut that does not contain the problem chemical (or chemicals).

To remain healthy, human beings, especially young people and the elderly, need to consume small amounts of substances known as vitamins and minerals. These substances are found in fresh foods, but some vitamins and minerals decay during storage or are destroyed during food preparation. Food technologists add carefully measured doses of vitamins and minerals to many foods to make the them as healthy as possible.

Vitamins and Minerals

Vitamins are chemicals that the body needs for certain tasks but cannot manufacture for itself. We need different quantities of each vitamin each day. Some vitamins are found in many foods, while others, such as vitamin D, are found only in milk, colorful vegetables, and fish. Minerals are usually chemical elements, such as iron and calcium. The body uses minerals to keep itself running properly. Iron, for example, is used to make blood **cells**, while calcium is used to make bone.

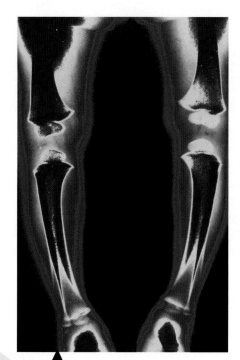

A colored X-ray shows the bowed legs of a child with **rickets**, a disease caused by a lack of vitamin D.

SCIENCE CONCEPTS

A Healthy Diet

There are at least fifteen vitamins (scientists are still unsure exactly how many types of vitamin B there are) and another seven vitaminlike substances that are equally important. Consuming the correct amounts of the right vitamins and minerals each day is not, by itself, a guarantee of good health, nor does it mean that a person is eating a healthy diet. Vitamins and minerals are only part of a healthy diet, which must include the right proportions of **protein**, fats, **carbohydrates**, fiber, water, and calories.

Diet Deficiencies

You can get all the necessary vitamins and minerals by eating a wide range of fresh foods, but this is not always easy, or even possible, in some countries. People whose diets consist mainly of processed rice may develop a disease called **beriberi**, which affects the nerves. Beriberi is caused by a lack of vitamin B1. Processed rice does not contain this crucial vitamin. People who do not eat enough fresh fruit may develop **scurvy**, caused by a deficiency (lack) of vitamin C. Scurvy can make people feel ill and cause their teeth to fall out. Technologists often add carefully measured doses of vitamins and minerals to **fortify** popular foods. Breakfast cereals, for example, have been fortified for nearly sixty years. In 1998, U.S. companies also began adding **folic acid** to cereal, pasta, bread, and flour. Folic acid helps reduce the number of babies born with brain and spinal-cord defects.

*Rice is a good source of **magnesium**, **niacin**, and vitamins E and B6. Processed rice lacks vitamin B1, which is vital for our nerves.*

Too Much of a Good Thing

The body requires only very small doses of vitamins and minerals. For some vitamins and minerals, the recommended daily dose is measured in millionths of a gram. In fact, some vitamins and minerals are poisonous when consumed in larger quantities. People who are very health conscious and take too many vitamin supplements in addition to the vitamins in their food run the risk of poisoning themselves.

SCIENCE SNAPSHOT

Cholesterol is a type of fat that is essential to the human body. It is found only in foods made from animal products. Too much of a certain kind of cholesterol in your blood can lead to heart disease. Food technologists have discovered that adding soy powder to foods can help lower the levels of the "bad" type of cholesterol in blood. Many people now add soy powder to their daily meals.

To help keep us healthy and full of energy, food technologists add vitamins and minerals to many kinds of foods.

Food scientists sometimes make food more useful by altering the food itself. Updated farming methods have already improved many food crops by increasing their productivity. **Genetic modification (GM)** of food crops allows food technologists to create plants with exactly the characteristics the technologists want them to have.

Genetic Modification

Almost every cell in every living thing contains a molecule called **DNA** (**deoxyribonucleic acid**), which consists of a series of chemically coded instructions called **genes**. Every species has its own particular set of genes, known as its **genome**. Genes vary from individual to individual. Genes decide how tall a person will grow, how good a person's eyesight is, and whether or not someone will suffer from certain diseases.

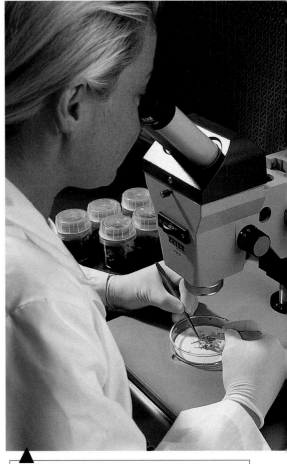

*A scientist dissects pieces of plant matter under a microscope in preparation for **gene splicing**.*

SCIENCE CONCEPTS

GM Food Safety Concerns

Laboratory tests have shown that GM versions of crops are perfectly safe for humans to eat, but safe consumption is not the only question. Some scientists are running tests to see if modified genes spread to other plants through wind-borne pollen. If that happens, weeds could soon become resistant to weed killers. Some environmental groups illegally protest against genetically modified food by destroying fields containing GM crops.

Scientists have learned how to extract DNA from cells and snip out a particular gene. They can then replace it with a different gene and put the DNA back into the cells. Sometimes called gene splicing, this process is used mainly in the medical and food industries. Gene splicing will not work on some plants. Instead, the modified DNA must be blasted into seeds on microscopic particles of gold in a technique known as "shot gunning."

GM Foods

Technologists have already produced GM versions of some crops, such as soybeans and corn. In some cases, plant genes have been altered to make the plants resistant to weed killers. Farmers can spray a whole field with weed killer and kill only the weeds. The GM crops remain unaffected. GM crops can grow larger than normal plants, and harvesting these crops is often easier and faster because farmers do not have to separate the weeds from the plants. GM crops are now grown in some countries and are used as ingredients in a wide variety of foods. Some of the people in both these and other countries, however, are concerned about the safety of GM crops and are demanding that all products containing GM ingredients be clearly labeled.

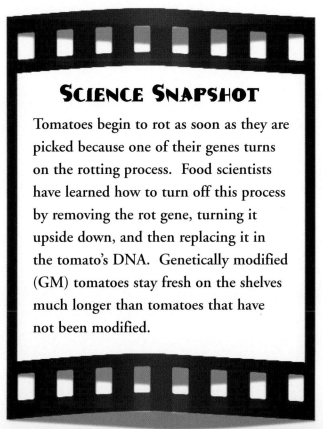

SCIENCE SNAPSHOT

Tomatoes begin to rot as soon as they are picked because one of their genes turns on the rotting process. Food scientists have learned how to turn off this process by removing the rot gene, turning it upside down, and then replacing it in the tomato's DNA. Genetically modified (GM) tomatoes stay fresh on the shelves much longer than tomatoes that have not been modified.

An ordinary tomato will decay in a matter of days. A genetically modified tomato will last up to twenty days longer.

Plant protein can be turned into a variety of different food products, from sandwich fillings to burgers.

Many people are **vegetarians,** which means they choose to not eat meat. This choice is usually because they have strong views about killing animals or because their religion forbids them to eat animals. Meat is a natural part of many diets, but it is not essential to human survival. The most difficult part of a vegetarian diet is making sure to get enough protein.

Plant Protein

Meat is a valuable source of protein and a typical ingredient in many meals. Using protein extracted from plants, food technologists have been able to create vegetarian "meat" that smells, tastes, and chews just like animal meat. Soybeans contain about 50 percent protein, so they are especially suitable as ingredients in meat substitutes. As the soybeans are processed, their protein is concentrated even more, until it is about 70 percent protein. This mixture can be flavored and treated to produce a variety of "meat" products.

The easiest product to make is vegetarian ground "meat." Soy protein is made into a stiff paste that breaks up into small pieces, or granules, that can be dried and added to recipes in place of ground meat. For chewier "meat," food technologists use a heat process that alters the protein and makes it chewier. The best quality vegetarian "meats," however, use a more complex process. Soy protein is spun into narrow fibers that are thinner than human hairs. These fibers can be knitted or woven, just like textile fibers, to produce vegetarian "meat" with nearly the same texture and mouthfeel as animal meat.

SCIENCE CONCEPTS

Types of Protein

Protein is an essential part of our diets, but our bodies do not care whether they get plant protein or animal protein, as long as they get enough protein. Animal protein is much more expensive to produce than vegetable protein because animals have to be fed and cared for until they are old enough to be slaughtered for their meat.

Traditional cheeses contain an animal by-product called rennet. It traps the milk fat that gives cheeses their flavor.

Vegetable "Cheese"

Cheese made from milk is a valuable source of protein so many vegetarians eat dairy products, such as milk and butter, but they will not eat cheeses made with a substance called **rennet**, which comes from the stomach lining of dead cows. Rennet helps extract the fat and protein from milk to make cheese.

Food technologists have developed a plant-based alternative to rennet that is used to make vegetarian cheeses. These products are usually found in a separate section of the grocery store or may be available through specialty health-food stores that carry vegetarian products.

SCIENCE SNAPSHOT

Many people enjoy the taste of bacon, but vegetarians and people whose religions do not allow them to eat pork will not eat bacon. Food technologists have developed bacon from beef cattle, turkeys, and vegetables that looks and tastes similar to bacon made from hogs.

Today, many people have trouble finding the time to cook a traditional meal from fresh ingredients. Food technologists make life easier by producing a range of prepared foods, such as ready-made sauces that can be served with pasta or rice. Even more convenient is an entire meal that is prepared and precooked. All the busy shopper needs to do is take it home and heat it properly in an oven or a microwave, and dinner is served.

Ready-made meals are not always a healthy option because they may contain large amounts of salt and fat.

Five-Star Chefs

Creating a ready-made meal is a tremendous challenge for food technologists. It sounds simple enough, but, in fact, it is a very complicated process that involves a team of people, each with his or her own specialization. Once the basic ingredients have been selected, technologists must spend days in the kitchen adjusting the amount of each of the ingredients to get the taste just right. Every time they make an adjustment, they keep a careful record so they know how they produced a particular flavor. If the ingredients must be cooked, the cooking times are measured to the second so they can repeat the same results time after time.

Made to Keep

Getting a ready-made meal to taste like it was made by a restaurant chef is only the first stage. Because these meals are not eaten right away, food technologists also must consider

SCIENCE CONCEPTS

Ready-Made Recipes

When you buy a ready-made meal, you are buying two things: the food and the storage and preparation instructions. Many ready-made meals require heating to a certain temperature for a particular length of time. To enjoy the meal, it's best to read and follow the directions. These instructions are not just suggestions. They should always be followed to help prevent an upset stomach or food poisoning.

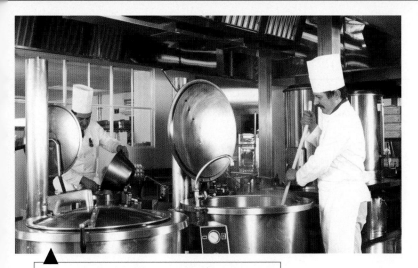

Ready-made meals are made in huge quantities.

the problem of storage. Most ready-made meals are sold refrigerated or frozen. Food technologists store sample meals for different lengths of time and then test them to see which flavors or qualities are affected. Recipes often need to be adjusted so the meals will store better. After technologists produce a meal that tastes good and stores well, they tackle the problems of mass producing the meal.

Mass Made

Ready-made meals are not made one at a time in a small kitchen. They are prepared and cooked by the thousands in large factories, where most of the workers never even see the completed product. Some of the workers may even be robots. Food technologists must discover the most efficient ways to make their meal in large numbers. They also have to make sure that ingredients are constantly checked for quality. Only when the first batch of meals leaves the factory is their task completed.

SCIENCE SNAPSHOT

Food technologists have an easier time getting a flavor exactly right than you do. Food cooked at home doesn't always taste exactly the same as the last time you made it. The flavorings you use for a single meal can be so small that it is impossible to measure them accurately. Or, you might be the kind of cook who flavors a dish "to taste" so it tastes exactly right to you. It is much easier to be accurate when dealing with larger quantities that are precisely measured in a factory.

Workers in a food factory monitor an assembly line. Hats and protective clothing help them maintain the highest level of cleanliness.

Case Study: A New Soft Drink

Soft drinks are big business. People around the world drink billions of cans and bottles of their favorite soft drinks each year. Developing a new product with an exciting and refreshing taste can take months, or even years. To create a new soft drink product, food technologists usually work as a team.

Research and Development

Research is the essential first stage of the process of drink creation. Consumers are asked what they like most about their favorite drinks and what they do not like about other drinks. Researchers may also ask about people's attitudes toward health and fitness. The information obtained from hundreds of interviews is used to decide the basic design of the new drink: its flavor, color, amount of **carbonation**, and whether it will contain sugar or artificial sweeteners. This drink design is then handed over to the drink technologists who decide exactly which ingredients to use. They will produce many versions of the drink, each with a slightly different combination of ingredients. All versions of the new drink will undergo a series of taste tests to determine the most popular flavor.

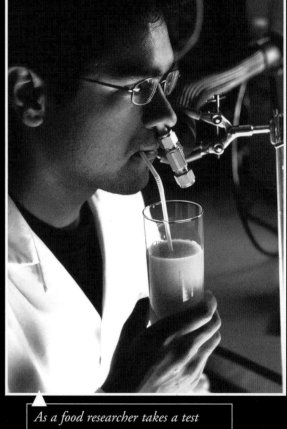

As a food researcher takes a test drink of orange juice, a nasal sensor detects flavor molecules in his nose.

Sometimes, friends like a certain brand of soft drink enough to share it.

Adding Bubbles

A process known as carbonation adds the sparkle to soft drinks. Carbon dioxide gas is forced into the drink under pressure so that it dissolves in the liquid. The gas will stay in the drink for as long as it is stored under pressure. When a can or bottle is opened for the first time, the pressure is released, and the carbon dioxide bubbles out of the liquid. These bubbles create the fizzy sensation in the mouth that many people enjoy. Carbonation, however, can affect the flavor of a drink's other ingredients so technologists have to be very careful to add exactly the right amount of fizz. Tasting sessions help them decide exactly how much carbonation to add to a drink.

Always the Same

Most people have a favorite soft drink because that particular drink always tastes exactly the same. They look forward to both quenching their thirst and enjoying that set of flavors. No matter where they are, they know that their favorite drink will always taste just the way they like it. The end result of the soft drink development process is not the drink itself but a detailed list of instructions for making that drink. These instructions are known as the drink's **formula**, and they are very precise. For example, it is not enough to simply list "water" in the formula. The taste of water from different localities varies slightly because of naturally occurring minerals. A drink's formula usually contains exact instructions about how the water should be treated.

Case Study Fact File

- **Careful, controlled research is the first stage of any food development project.**
- **When experimenting with different flavors, it is very important to keep an accurate record of the ingredients that are used.**
- **Carbonation is the name of the process that makes soft drinks bubbly, or sparkling.**
- **The bubbles in a sparkling drink are an important part of its taste.**
- **Each soft drink has its own unique formula, or precise instructions, on how to prepare the drink.**

This researcher is monitoring water quality in a beverage factory. The type and quality of water used must be consistent every time the product is tested.

French fries are one of the most popular foods in the world. Millions of them are eaten every day. Some french fries are prepared and cooked by hand, using traditional methods, but most are now made by machines in modern factories. Machines are widely used in the food industry because they are reliable and efficient. Some foods, including french fries, can be prepared with hardly any human assistance.

Only large potatoes are turned into french fries.

Handling

Making french fries by hand takes both time and care. Each potato must be washed, peeled, and then carefully cut with a knife, first into slices, and then into rectangular strips that are ready for the pan. Inside a factory, machines designed by food technologists use some very unusual methods to achieve pan-ready fries. Fresh potatoes are unloaded into large tanks of water that are about the same size as a public swimming pool. Rocks and soil sink to the bottom of the tank, while the potatoes float at the surface. The potatoes are then washed across a series of screens that filter out those that are too small for making french fries. The potatoes that make the grade are moved along a series of water channels and onto **conveyor belts**.

Peeling

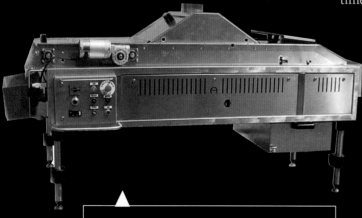

Water-gun knives like this one can cut french fries at a faster rate than any person could.

Removing the skin from a potato by hand is very time consuming. It is much easier to use simple steam-powered science. As the potato moves along the conveyor belt, it is blasted with high-temperature steam for a few seconds. The steam causes water underneath the potato's skin to boil. As the boiling water turns to steam, it expands very rapidly, and the potato's skin is literally blown off by the force of the expansion. The freshly "peeled" potato then continues along the conveyor belt, while its skin is collected for animal feed.

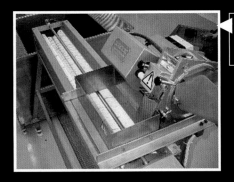

This machine sorts peeled potatoes quickly.

Cutting

When producing french fries in large quantities, it is important that all fries have the same width and depth so that they will cook evenly. Cutting one potato into equally sized fries is hard enough to do. Imagine having to cut hundreds of thousands of potatoes each day. Factories that produce french fries use one of the most ingenious machines in the entire food industry: the water-gun knife. This machine does something that human workers just cannot do. It uses a jet of high-pressure water to shoot potatoes through a metal grid at about 81 miles (130 km) per hour. The grid edges are made of razor-sharp blades. As the potatoes blast through the grid, the blades cut them neatly into french fries of the required size.

Computer Control

All the machines that are used for sorting, peeling, and cutting potatoes are controlled by computers that keep the conveyor belts moving at the correct speeds. Throughout the process, electronic sensors monitor quality control. These sensors can detect tiny differences in color, and any imperfect french fries are quickly removed from the conveyor belt by mechanical arms. After being cut, the fries are dried by hot-air blowers before being cooked in oil in automatic frying machines. The french fries are then cooled and frozen for distribution.

Case Study Fact File

- **High-speed machines in large factories produce most french fries.**
- **Inside a factory, potatoes move at speeds of up to 81 miles (130 km) per hour.**
- **Machines use high-temperature steam to remove potato skins.**
- **Potatoes are cut into equal-sized french fries by a machine called a water-gun knife.**
- **Electronic sensors scan the french fries before cooking to detect any imperfections.**

In spite of the health risks connected with eating too much fat, fries remain a popular food.

Case Study: Tasty Snacks

Crispy, crunchy snacks are very popular foods. A combination of crispiness and strong flavor makes snack foods fun to eat. Food technologists work hard to create exciting new flavors and to make their products more tasty. One way to improve flavors is to add more salt to the ingredients. Some people, however, believe that snack foods already contain too much salt.

Snack Production

Potato chips, which are very thin slices of potatoes that are fried until they are golden brown and crunchy, are one of the original snack foods. While potato chips are still made this way, the majority of snack foods are not made from sliced vegetables. The main ingredient of most snacks is flour — usually potato flour, corn flour, or rice flour. The flour is mixed with water into a thick paste to which flavorings and other ingredients are added. The paste is then rolled, pressed, molded, or squirted into a wide variety of shapes. Air can also be bubbled through the paste to make the final product even crunchier. After cooking, additional flavoring is often added before the snacks are packaged.

Salt

The word "salt" usually refers to table salt, which is the common name for the naturally occurring chemical **sodium chloride**. People have been adding salt to their food for thousands of years. It is the oldest of all food flavorings. Saltiness is one of the basic tastes detected by the tongue, but the main reason it is added to food is that salt makes other flavors taste better. Salt is a flavor **enhancer**. Most cookbook recipes include at least a "pinch" of salt among their ingredients, and most prepared foods contain added salt. Snack foods usually contain considerably more than a pinch of salt. Our bodies need a little salt each day to remain healthy, but many people eat far more salt than they need. Some researchers believe that eating too much salt can lead to illness. Medical experts also have become concerned about the amount of salt people eat.

- Potato chips are one of the original snack food.
- Most snack foods contain salt, which is essential to life, but too much salt may be harmful.
- Salt is a flavor enhancer because it makes other flavors taste better.
- People, especially young people, can become "addicted" to salty foods and snacks.
- Chemical salts other than sodium chloride are often used as flavor enhancers for snack foods.

A bowl of potato chips contains a considerable amount of salt, which may not be healthy.

Crammed with Flavor

Most snack foods have strong flavors. Some are flavored with uncooked ingredients such as cheese, onion, or garlic. Some have cooked flavors, such as fried bacon or roast beef, while others have mainly hot flavors, such as chili. Snack foods often have special flavor formulas that include both natural and laboratory-made ingredients. No matter what kinds and how many flavorings are used, however, you can be almost certain that your snack food contains salt.

Salt is found in deposits left behind from evaporated seawater.

Case Study: A Totally New Food

Perhaps the most exciting and important work carried out by food technologists is the development of new sources of food. One of these new food sources is mycoprotein, which is used as a meat substitute. The advantage of mycoprotein is that it is not produced on farms, where it can be affected by bad weather. Instead, it is "grown" inside steel tanks in a factory.

A scientist examines fungus samples in the laboratory. Scientists developing mycoprotein had to figure out the best way to produce it in large quantities.

From the Soil

Mycoprotein is neither animal nor vegetable. It is made from a tiny, single-celled fungus that lives in soil. The fungus, which has a high protein content, was discovered in the 1960s after scientists began a worldwide search for alternative sources of protein. The discovery was just the first step toward developing a new food. Technologists had to learn how to grow the fungus in a laboratory so that it could be fully tested. When they were sure that the mycoprotein was safe to eat, they had to develop a method of producing it in large quantities. Meanwhile, other technologists experimented with ways of flavoring the new food. The commercial production of mycoprotein began in the mid-1980s.

Nonstop Production

As with most single-celled organisms, mycoprotein can be grown outside its natural **habitat** in a mixture, or "**culture**," of water, sugar, and minerals. This method is mainly used in laboratories to produce identical quantities of a substance. Producing large quantities of mycoprotein requires culturing on a large scale in huge stainless-steel tanks. Under ideal conditions, the amount of fungus doubles every five hours. It is "harvested" continuously by mechanical filters and is then ready for flavoring and packing.

Mycoprotein burgers were introduced in Europe in 1985, but were not approved for sale in the United States until 2002.

Food Products

Mycoprotein's individual fungus cells are shaped like tiny threads. These threads give mycoprotein a very good basic texture so there is no need to process it into fibers as is sometimes done with soy protein. Food technologists have used their skills to flavor mycoprotein so that its taste resembles meats such as chicken, turkey, ham, and beef. Mycoprotein can be used instead of these meats in a wide variety of recipes, and it is available in the shapes of both burgers and sausages. There are even mycoprotein cold cuts that can be sliced and used to make sandwiches. Food products containing mycoprotein have been sold in Europe for about two decades, and they are now available in most other parts of the world as well.

Mycoprotein is sold under many brand names. It can be flavored and shaped to imitate various meats.

Glossary

allergy: a medical condition in which a person's body has a very strong defense reaction, such as sneezing or a rash, to an otherwise harmless substance, such as dust, pet hair, or peanuts.

bacteria: single-celled organisms that are found in every environment, from the bottom of the sea to inside our bodies. Most bacteria are harmless, but some kinds can cause food to go bad, and a few types can cause diseases.

beriberi: a disease that affects the nervous system, caused by a lack of vitamin B_1.

carbohydrates: the sugars, starches, and cellulose that come mostly from green plants and which the body uses for energy.

carbon dioxide: a colorless and odorless gas that is naturally present in the air in small quantities.

carbonation: the process of forcing carbon dioxide gas into a liquid under pressure. When the pressure is released, the gas bubbles out of the liquid, making it fizzy.

cells: the "building-blocks" of living things. Cells are the smallest units of an organism.

cholesterol: a waxy molecule that is a part of the membrane of every cell. It helps distribute fats and controls fatty buildup in blood vessels throughout the body, especially near the heart.

conveyor belts: continuous loops of fabric, plastic, or rubber laid over a series of rollers to form a constantly moving surface on which objects can be transported from one place to another.

culture: an artificially created habitat, made of water, sugar, and minerals, for growing controlled amounts of organisms that are used for research or to produce products.

defense mechanism: a bodily reaction that protects against or lessens harm to an organism.

diabetes: a disease (*diabetes mellitus*) that affects the body's ability to process carbohydrates such as sugar and starch.

diabetics: people who suffer from diabetes.

DNA (deoxyribonucleic acid): a molecule found in most body cells, which carries coded information in the form of genes.

emulsifier: a substance that allows two different liquids, such as water and oil, to mix by breaking up the oil into tiny droplets that stay evenly distributed throughout the solution (called an emulsion).

enhancer: an added substance that improves the quality of an original substance in some way.

ferment: to chemically change molecules of sugar into alcohol, producing carbon dioxide gas as a waste product.

folic acid: one of the B vitamins essential for growth and the proper production of red blood cells.

formula: the precise instructions, including a detailed list of ingredients, for making a particular substance or product.

fortify: to make stronger or more effective, as when vitamins are added to a food in order to provide more health benefits to the body.

fungi: organisms that are neither plant nor animal. Fungi grow somewhat like plants but do not need sunlight. Mushrooms, molds, and yeasts are the most common kinds of fungi.

gene splicing: inserting a gene into a certain place on a DNA molecule.

genes: coded instructions contained within DNA molecules that affect a particular characteristic of an organism, such as eye color.

genetic modification (GM): the process of artificially arranging an organism's genome.

genome: the complete instructions for creating a new organism.

gluten: a mixture of insoluble plant proteins in cereal grains, especially corn and wheat, which helps make dough sticky and elastic.

habitat: the particular environmental conditions in which an organism lives.

herbicides: poisons that kill plants.

irradiated: exposed to or treated with radiation.

lactose: a form of sugar that is naturally present in milk.

lactose-intolerant: unable to digest lactose.

lecithin: a widely used emulsifier that is a common ingredient in chocolate products.

magnesium: a silver-white, light metallic element that occurs abundantly in nature, such as in bones. It also helps with nerve function.

microbes: very tiny living organisms.

minerals: chemical elements, such as calcium, iron, and sodium, that the body requires in very small quantities.

molecules: the smallest chemical units of a particular substance, composed of one or more atoms.

mouthfeel: a term used by the food industry to describe the sensations felt by the tongue, teeth, and mouth parts when food is placed in the mouth.

mycoprotein: an edible protein obtained from a fungus and used to make food substitutes, especially for meat products.

niacin: an acid of the vitamin B complex, present in meat, wheat germ, and dairy products.

oxidation: the process by which a substance is changed in contact with oxygen, such as iron forming rust or a cut apple turning brown.

oxygen: a colorless, odorless gas that is naturally present in the atmosphere.

pasteurization: a heat treatment, developed by French scientist Louis Pasteur in the 1860s, that kills harmful microbes in milk and other liquids.

pollen: very fine plant dust, essential to the plant's reproduction.

protein: the main part of many foods that help build new body cells and repair old ones.

radiation: the energy emitted by certain types of atoms in the form of waves or particles.

receptors: specialized cells (such as the nerve cells that line the inside passages of the nose and detect flavor molecules) that detect miniscule amounts of different chemicals in the body.

rennet: a substance found in the stomachs of nursing calves and the stomach linings of adult cows that helps turn milk into cheese.

rickets: a disease caused by a vitamin D deficiency, which can result in soft, deformed bones.

scurvy: a disease caused by a vitamin C deficiency, which can result in bone and joint problems and tooth loss.

sodium chloride: the chemical name for table salt.

technologists: professionals who use scientific or technical knowledge to solve problems and develop new products.

texture: the feel, such as smoothness or roughness, of a substance.

ultra-heat-treated (UHT): a preservation method that uses extreme heat to kill organisms that can cause food to spoil and allows for unrefrigerated storage.

vegetarians: people who will not eat any meat or meat products.

vitamins: chemical substances essential for good health, found in fresh food and, to a lesser extent, in processed foods.

Index